ROMARE BEARDEN

Collage of Memories

By Jan Greenberg

Harry N. Abrams, Inc., Publishers

Painted paper scissored into shapes. Scraps of fabric. Hands cut from a photograph. Bits and pieces pasted on a board. This collage *Early Carolina Morning* recalls a scene in the South almost a hundred years ago. It was composed from memory by the artist Romare Bearden. His pictures are filled with images of everyday life as he lived it. Roosters, cats, guitars, trains, snakes, sunsets, and people were some of his favorite subjects.

Early Carolina Morning, 1978, Profile/Part I: The Twenties series, collage on board, 29 x 41 inches, private collection

When we look at his paintings, we feel we could be right there with him running through a cotton field in North Carolina or sitting on the front stoop of a tenement in Harlem. His art celebrates the struggles and triumphs of African American life in the twentieth century. Step inside Bearden's world, where jazz, rhythm, and blues meet a kaleidoscope of shimmering, shimmying colors.

Great-grandfather Kennedy hoisted three-year-old Romie (as everyone called him) high on his shoulders. Off they went to the station to watch the trains whizzing by. A crowd had gathered there, as the funeral train for Mrs. Stonewall Jackson, the wife of the Confederate general, slowly passed by. Great-grandfather held Romie up to see the railroad car carrying the coffin strewn with flowers and surrounded by soldiers. Watching the trains steam in and out of town was one of Romie's favorite pastimes. "All aboard for the New York and Atlanta Special!" He loved to hear the conductor shouting out the names of the cities. Romie and his great-grandfather would make up stories about who might be traveling on the train, where they might be heading. Lining the tracks were cotton mills that filled the air with a constant rumble of machinery processing cotton.

Romie and his mother, Bessye, circa 1920

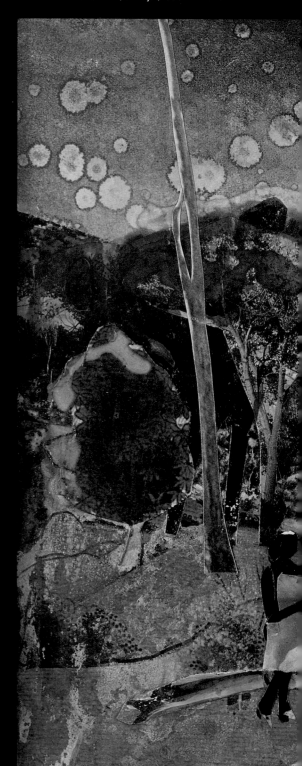

Photograph of Romie between his great-grandparents; standing, from left to right, his aunt Anna, mother and father, and his grandmother Cattie, 1917

8

Romie never forgot the sounds of his childhood—the roar of the engine pulling into town, the train whistles, a rooster's crowing, gospel singers, or guitars. But it was the visual images that remained most vivid in his mind.

Heavy Freight/Mecklenburg Evening, 1982, collage/acrylic, 7 $^1/_2$ x 11 $^5/_8$ inches, Estate of Romare Bearden

9

Above: *Mecklenburg Autumn*, 1979, lithograph, 27 x 21 ¹/₄ inches, Estate of Romare Bearden

Opposite: *Dinner Before the Revival Meeting*, 1978, Profile/Part I: Mecklenburg County series, collage, 7 x 10 ³/₄ inches, private collection

Romie was born in the white, wood frame "big house" of his father's grandparents. The Kennedys lived in the bustling town of Charlotte, North Carolina, the seat of Mecklenburg County. Framed by a wraparound porch and wide veranda, the "big house" stood on a corner across the yard from their grocery store. Romie and his parents, Bessye and Howard, lived down the street. From their window they could see the trestle leading to the main train station. It was 1911, the beginning of the great migration of African Americans leaving the South, riding the trains up North to find work.

With blond curly hair and blue eyes, Romie grew to be the "fair-haired boy" of the family, doted on but not spoiled. Outgoing and curious like his mother Bessye, Romie could charm apples off the trees.

As a child, Romie spent his days roaming the neighborhood and exploring the country-side. He played ball with his cousin Spinky on the steps of the Old Mint, where they used to make gold coins. He went to band concerts on Saturdays and church on Sundays, where his father played the organ. Quilting bees, cotton picking, revival meetings, and picnics—all formed the memories he would later turn into art.

The people Romie knew in Charlotte later became the subjects for hundreds of collages, including these two portraits of a woman named Maudell Sleet working in her garden. He said, "It didn't look anything like her. I tried to give it my feeling instead of making an exact likeness."

Maudell Sleet's Magic Garden, 1978, Profile/Part I: The Twenties series (Mecklenburg County), collage on board, 10 1/8 x 7 inches, private collection

Sunset and Moonrise with Maudell Sleet, 1978, collage on board, 41 x 29 inches, private collection

Born into slavery, Romie's great-grandparents, Rosa and Henry Kennedy, gained their freedom after the Civil War. They first worked as servants for the family of a man who was to become president of the United States, Woodrow Wilson. By 1914, the Kennedys had become successful, well-respected citizens of Charlotte, owning several houses and a grocery store. But times were changing in the South due to new laws that further separated white and black Americans—different schools, divided sections on buses, and other unfair—and unequal—rules of segregation.

One day Howard and Bessye took three-year-old Romie for a drive to go shopping in the white section of town. While his father stayed with him in their horse-drawn carriage, Bessye went into a store. Howard left Romie for a moment to look in a shop window. As he stepped back to the carriage, people on the street began pointing. The dark-skinned man approaching the blond child must be a kidnapper, they said. Bessye ran out of the store just in time to straighten things out. This upsetting incident made a strong impression on Romie's parents. They wanted their son to be raised in a place where differences between people were respected rather than feared. Would they find such a place in America?

Family, 1980, collage on board, 28 x 20 inches, Smithsonian American Art Museum, Washington, D.C.

Before long, Romie and his parents packed up and left the South for good, eventually settling in New York City. There on the streets of Harlem and at school, Romie met people from many other ethnic groups, including Irish, Italian, and Jewish immigrants from Europe. It seemed as if everyone was from somewhere else, looking for a better life. Later Romie would express this yearning to belong in America through his collages of Harlem.

The Street, 1964, photomontage, 31 x 40 inches, private collection

As he grew up, Romie often went back and forth between New York, Charlotte, Pittsburgh, and Baltimore to visit his grandparents. One summer when he was about ten, he stayed with his father's mother Cattie in Lutherville, a country town near Baltimore, Maryland. Her neighbor Mrs. Johnson, who still baked with the tin pans her grandmother used as a slave in the South, made a special cake that looked just like a watermelon. Swirls of red batter, seeds made of hand-cut chocolate chips, green-striped icing topped off with a sugary glaze—Mrs. Johnson's watermelon cake was in great demand.

Every Saturday Romie filled his wagon with freshly baked cakes to deliver house to house to wealthy folks in town. Mrs. Johnson's husband, a blind folksinger, would go along, strumming his guitar with one hand, holding onto Romie's with the other. One afternoon they stopped by the side of the road so Romie could fill a pail with blackberries to bring back to Mrs. Johnson. Mr. Johnson sat on a tree stump and plucked his guitar. The tunes he played were like nothing Romie had ever heard before. Mr. Johnson made up his own music, saying his sounds came from the wind moving through his fingers on the strings.

In *Mr. Jeremiah's Sunset Guitar* and *Three Folk Musicians*, guitar players strum their folksy blues, recreating the days a young boy wandered through country fields listening to Mr. Johnson's music and picking ripe berries.

Billows of gray smoke. Thundering furnaces. Shrill factory whistles. This was Pittsburgh in the 1920s, center of the steel industry. Romie's grandmother Carrie Banks, Bessye's mother, ran a boardinghouse for steel mill workers, many of whom had migrated there from the South to find better paying jobs. As a teenager, staying with his grandmother, Romie often saw the men return home, their skin scorched from the fiery blasts.

Above: *Mill Hand's Lunch Bucket*, 1978, Profile/Part I: The Twenties, collage on board,
13 ³/₄ x 18 ¹/₈ inches, Estate of Romare Bearden

Opposite: *Allegheny Morning Sky*, 1978, Pittsburgh Memories: Profile/Part II, collage,
10 ⁷/₈ x 14 ¹/₂ inches, private collection

One summer day in Pittsburgh, Romie was shooting marbles in the backyard with his friend Dennis and cousin Spinky from Charlotte. Out of nowhere a boy with braces on his legs hobbled over to the edge of the yard. He didn't say a word, just stood there, watching them. Dennis started teasing him and soon the boys were beating up on him. "Miss Carrie", who spotted the scuffle from her kitchen window, ran out shaking her broom to rescue the new boy. His name was Eugene and soon, said Romie, "He got to be our friend." It turned out Eugene knew how to draw. Miss Carrie set up a table so he could give Romie lessons. On sheets of brown paper Eugene would sketch the boarding-house where he lived with his mother a few blocks away. By leaving out the front of the house he exposed the goings-on inside—half-dressed women, dancing, and drinking.

He even drew a shooting. When Miss Carrie saw the drawings, she was so shocked that she threw them into the furnace and marched straight over to Eugene's house to pack up his clothes. For a while Eugene moved into Miss Carrie's, along with his pet doves and pigeons. A year later the frail boy died. Romie never forgot Eugene, and in his homage painting *Farewell Eugene*, he recalled his funeral.

Later in collages picturing the conflict and strife of African Americans living in Harlem, a dense city neighborhood of New York, he too stripped away the facades of buildings to reveal what was happening inside.

Above: *The Block*, 1971 (detail), collage of cut and pasted paper on masonite, 48 x 216 inches, Metropolitian Museum of Art, New York

Opposite: *Farewell Eugene*, 1978, Profile/Part I: The Twenties, collage on board, 16 $^1/_4$ x 20 $^1/_2$ inches, private collection

By the 1930s, Romie's energetic and capable mother Bessye had become well-known in Harlem for her work as a newspaper editor and as a political activist for African Americans, especially women. Romie's father Howard worked as a sanitation inspector for the New York Health Department. From actors to writers to politicians and musicians, anyone who was anybody in Harlem stopped by the Beardens' apartment. Romie would come home from school to find the poet Langston Hughes or the bandleader Duke Ellington sitting in his living room, surrounded by Bessye's ten or more Siamese cats. It was the heyday of jazz, and Romie haunted the nearby honky-tonks and dance halls. "You had to get with the music," he said. "The clothes you wore, the way you talked . . . everything you did was, you might say, geared to groove." Jazz inspired him to make some of his most colorful paintings.

Show Time, 1974, Of the Blues series, collage with acrylic and lacquer on board, 50 x 40 inches, private collection

Romie was good at anything he tried to do. A star pitcher on an all-black baseball team in college, he was encouraged to try out for the major leagues. But there were no African American players in big-league baseball in those days. A coach told him he could pass for white, but Romie, who had been taught to fight against prejudice, refused.

Besides, he was more interested in drawing. His witty cartoons had appeared regularly in his college humor magazine. There was one problem. Bessye and Howard expected Romie to become a doctor, not an artist. But Romie also had been taught to be true to himself. After college, he enrolled in art classes at night. To support himself, he took a day job as a caseworker for the welfare department, helping poor gypsy families who had emigrated to New York from Eastern Europe. Sympathy for his clients and the hard lives they endured would be expressed later in artworks. Sad faces with puzzled looks and accusing eyes confront the viewer in this collage called *110th Street.* The photographs are of real people cut out of magazines. "Putting the photograph in a different space than you saw it in the magazine," Romie said, "can have another meaning entirely."

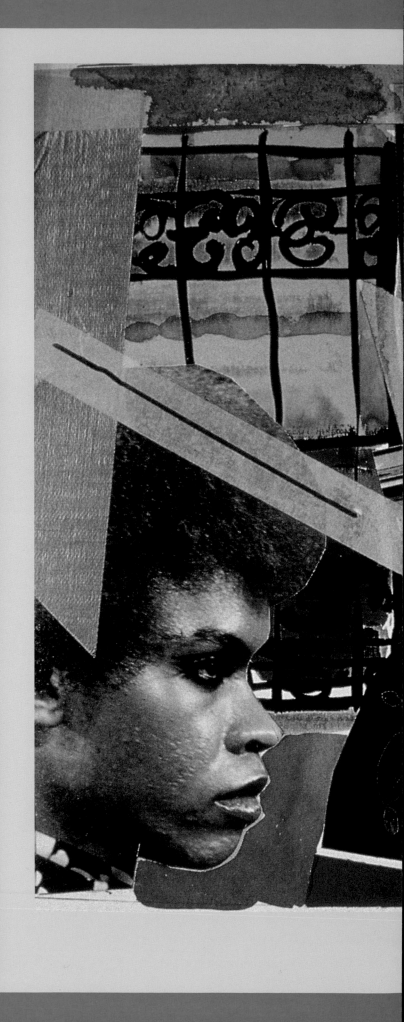

110th Street (n.d.), collage on paper, 14 x 22 inches, private collection

In 1940, Romie finally rented his first art studio in Harlem, setting up an easel with paintbrushes and oils. He tacked brown paper on the easel and there it sat blank week after week. Romie had a case of "artist's block," which meant he was stuck. A woman named Ida came to clean his studio every Saturday. One of Romie's friends said she was so ugly that "she looked like a locomotive coming around a corner."

One day Ida asked him if the empty sheet of brown paper was the same one she had seen on that wooden stand the week before. "I don't know what to paint," Romie admitted.

Artist with Painting and Model, 1981, Profile/Part II: The Thirties series,
collage on board, 44 x 56 inches, private collection

Patchwork Quilt, 1970, collage on board, 35 ³/₄ x 47 ⁷/₈ inches,
Museum of Modern Art, New York

"Why don't you paint me?" she asked. He stared at her with surprise. "I know what I look like, but when you look and find what's beautiful in me, then you're going to be able to do something on that paper of yours." Romie said, "It got me started thinking about people I knew and remembered down South." He began painting scenes recalling the Charlotte of his memory, experimenting with an opaque watercolor medium called gouache. Ida inspired him to work from live models, and his interest in painting the African American female figure continued throughout his career.

In the 1950s, the fashion in the New York art world was a style
of painting with dashing lines, thick paint, and no recognizable
subject matter, called Abstract Expressionism. These big, brash
works were causing a stir all over the United States and Europe.
Romie, never a follower of the latest trends, had his own ideas.
The abstract paintings he made were soft and quiet with thinned-
out washes of color, the texture of the sky. But eventually Romie
realized he could not say what he wanted to say, "to paint the life
of my people as I know it," without a realistic subject. Unable to
support himself with his art, Romie started writing songs. One of
his compositions, "Seabreeze," rose to the top of the record
charts. How can you waste your life, a friend asked him, when
you don't believe in what you're doing? Romie knew he was right.
Somehow he had lost his way. One night at a party he met a
talented young dancer named Nanette Rohan. They fell in love
and got married. She convinced him to get back to painting again.

Mountains of the Moon, 1956, oil on canvas, 40 $\frac{1}{2}$ x 31 inches, private collection

In the summer of 1963, 200,000 people marched on Washington, D.C., to demand equal rights for African Americans. Television and newspapers flashed pictures of the march across the country. In New York, African American artists joined together to help the cause. The group named themselves "Spiral" to indicate a starting point that would move in all directions, especially upward. The Spiral group wanted to be accepted as artists in their own right, without reference to their color. But they also wanted to respect their heritage, to make a difference.

Cotton, 1964, photomontage, 39 x 49 ⁵/₈ inches, Smithsonian American Art Museum, Washington, D.C.

Mysteries, 1964, photomontage, 49 x 61 ¹/₂ inches, Estate of Romare Bearden

At one of their meetings, Romie brought in a large sack filled with hundreds of photographs he had collected and cut in various shapes. Spreading them out on the floor, he suggested the group make a large mural together. The other artists lost interest in the project, but it gave Romie a great idea. Back at his studio he carefully pasted down the photos clipped from magazines onto small boards. Then he photographically enlarged the collages, mounting them on masonite boards.

Called photomontages, these large black-and-white pictures were based on his childhood memories of Mecklenburg County, Pittsburgh and Harlem. Photos of oversized heads, as seen in *Cotton* and *Mysteries*, seem to project themselves right out to the viewer. He named this powerful new series Projections.

When the photomontages were exhibited, the series was hailed as a great success. After years of experimenting, Romie finally had made a breakthrough, finding a style that felt right, that expressed what he needed to say. Through his collages, he would document the history and culture of people that he felt had long been ignored. Some found his street scenes raw and fearful, but no other American artist had given such a powerful voice to those who had not been heard. He said, "Art celebrates a victory . . . it involves conquering and redeeming both the beauty and sullenness of the past . . . it proclaims that black people have survived in spite of everything."

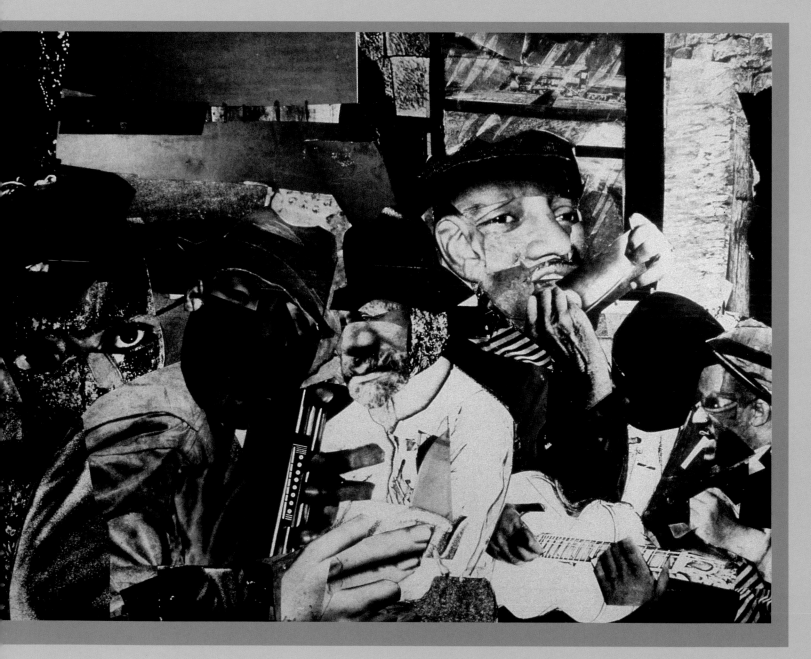

Above: *Train Whistle Blues I*, 1964, photomontage, 29 x 37 $^1/_2$ inches, Estate of Romare Bearden

Opposite: *Conjur Woman*, 1964, collage of paper and polymer paint on board, 9 $^1/_2$ x 7 inches, private collection

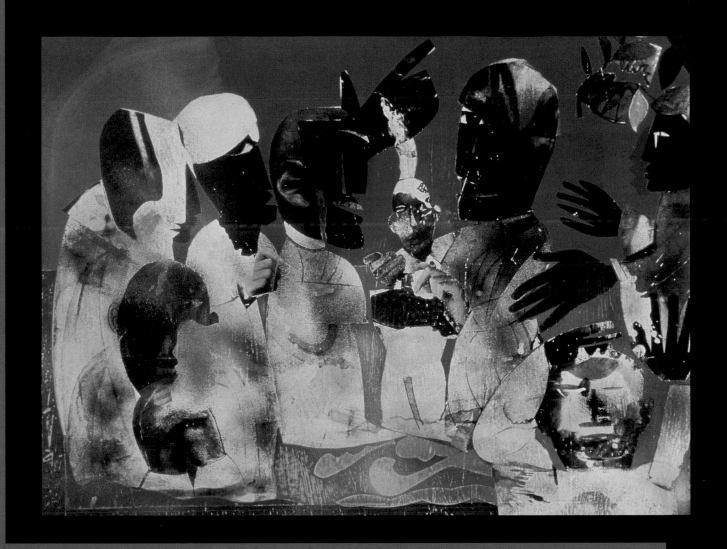

In his studio, Romie played jazz recordings. Jazz provided him with "continuous finger-snapping head-shaking enjoyment." But it also filled him with new ideas. He listened to the songs of the female ballad singers who sang of lost love and heartbreak. "Even though you go through these terrible experiences, you come out feeling good—life will prevail," Romie said.

He paid special attention to the silences or pauses between the notes in jazz, especially on the piano. "I listened and listened until I couldn't hear the music, only the silences." The contrast of hot and cold colors seen in his collages is similar to the pauses heard in jazz. The artist learned to improvise like the musicians, finding a structure for his picture, then letting himself go from there.

Colors and shapes pop and pulsate in a staccato rhythm in this collage called *The Blues.* As he worked and reworked the picture, Romie was involved in the process, in achieving a certain effect, rather than trying to imitate real life.

Above: *Carolina Shout*, 1974, Of the Blues series, collage with acrylic & lacquer on board, 37 $^1/_2$ x 51 inches, Mint Museum of Art, North Carolina

Opposite: *The Blues*, 1974, collage with acrylic and lacquer on board, 24 x 18 inches, Honolulu Academy of Art, Hawaii

Church music and street sounds filled a gallery at the Museum of Modern Art in New York City. A major exhibition of works by Romare Bearden! It was 1971 and the artist was fifty-nine years old. Long considered one of America's greatest "black" artists, his recognition as a great artist without labels came later. From paintings to collages, print-making to mosaics and watercolors, he experimented with new techniques all his life. One of his missions, when he became successful, was to encourage younger African American

The Block, 1971 (detail), collage of cut and pasted paper on masonite, 48 x 216 inches, Metropolitian Museum of Art, New York

artists. He helped fund the Cinque gallery in New York City to showcase their work. He loved giving advice to the students who flocked to his studio. "I think the artist has to be something like a whale, swimming with his mouth wide open, absorbing everything until he has what he really needs. When he finds that, he can start to make limitations. And then he really begins to grow."

A few years later, high above the turquoise sea on the Caribbean island of St. Martin, the birthplace of Nanette's family, the Beardens built a simple white house and studio. There, with his striped cat Gyppo roaming in and out of his studio, Romie started a new series. He had moved away from using photographs in favor of painted paper. The pictures were based on the energy he felt from the natives who lived on the island. The islanders practiced an old-time religion from West Africa called Obeah. They believed in magic, surrounding their festivals in a cloak of secrecy. But as they got to know the gentle bear of a man with the hearty laugh who quietly observed things with a sense of wonder, they came to trust him. They invited Romie to witness their ceremonies. Tropical in feeling with bright colors and flowing shapes, these dappled watercolors show fishing villages, sugarcane fields, snakes, birds, lush foliage, and people at work, play or, rest.

Obeah High Priestess, 1984, watercolor on paper, 29 $^7/_8$ x 21 $^1/_4$ inches, private collection

Blue Snake, 1971, private collection

By the time Romare Bearden died in 1988 at age seventy-six, he had received many honors, including the National Medal of Arts, and had been showcased in dozens of galleries and museums all over the country. He kept painting up until the day he went into the hospital for the last time.

Palm Sunday Procession, 1967-1968, collage, 56 x 44 inches, Hood Museum, New Hampshire

The Carnival Begins, 1984, watercolor and collage, 22 ¹/₂ x 30 inches, Estate of Romare Bearden

Although Romare Bearden's art found its roots in African American culture, it is an art that speaks to everyone. Calling and recalling voices from our shared memories, Romie's people—sitting, standing, strutting, strumming, singing, and shouting—cast their spells, celebrate life.

Studio Visit with Romie

How did Romie make his collages? Dressed in workman's overalls, he stood at a table scattered with painted paper, pens, markers, brushes, scraps of fabric, and clippings from books and magazines. He began by pasting down rectangles of color, usually on a board. On top of that, he layered bits and pieces of photographic images—African masks, animal eyes, plants, or faces, arms, and hands, all taken out of context and rearranged together. A master with a scissors, he expertly cut paper, slicing it in quick, deft strokes. He also tore sections of the paper away. After pasting and pressing the cut images onto a board, he might add paint with a brush or lines with a pen for color or shading. It was not a simple process. Sometimes if he didn't press hard enough, bubbles appeared on the glued surface. Large collages on heavy masonite board would fall off the wall. Canvas could warp. Romie's art was the result of years of testing and trying.

Photograph by Marvin E. Newman

In *The Piano Lesson*, the overlapping rectangles of blue, red, and orange produce an effect of flatness. The teacher and her pupil look posed and still. The artist pasted down bits of cloth, wood, and advertising images from an old catalog to decorate this old-fashioned Southern parlor.

The Piano Lesson, 1983, Mecklenburg Autumn series, oil with collage, 40 x 30 inches, private collection

Family Dinner, 1968, collage on board, 30 x 40 inches, Toledo Museum of Art, Ohio

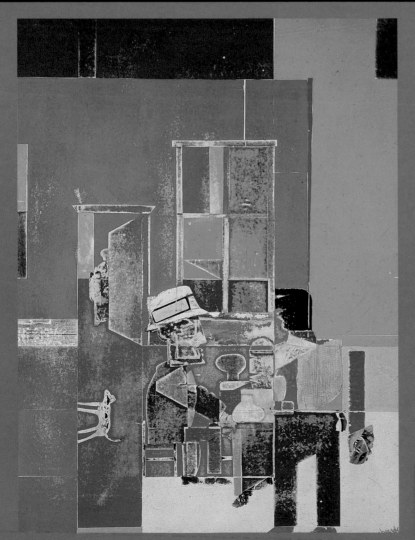

Whether Romie began with an idea in his head or not, he improvised, or made it up as he went along. By the time he built up a patchwork of paint and paper, a whole new scene might emerge. "People begin to come. Some are sitting; some are playing; a lady cooking. You have to enchant memory. You are not working like a photographer." In every painting, he said, the artist must find something to set him free. Romie called his way of making art "putting something over something else."

Carolina Blue, 1969, collage on panel, 40 x 30 inches, Estate of Romare Bearden

Author's Note

Although I never had the opportunity to meet Romare Bearden, I was fortunate enough to find many first-hand accounts of his life. Records of his artworks, his library, and papers have been preserved at the Romare Bearden Foundation in New York City, where I spent time doing research and talking to family members about their impressions of this generous, gifted man. His wife Nanette's sister, Sheila Rohan, remembers him as a Southern gentlemen. Kind, intelligent, he reminded her of a college professor. Their mother liked him, thought he was just right for one of her eight daughters. Although the Beardens never had children of their own, they were devoted to their three nieces, who used to ride the train into the city on weekends to visit. His niece, the artist Diedra Harris-Kelley, said their Canal Street apartment and studio were always open, with a continuous flow of people stopping by. She described books laying open on tables and Duke Ellington or Earl Hines records invariably playing in the background. Romie believed music and literature informed his art. I can picture him there on Canal Street, surrounded by friends and family, cats, books, music, and materials, sharing his stories, an artist at ease with his life and his craft. And standing before his collages and watercolors, I find myself looking beyond his personal experience to a place that can be shared by everyone. Finally, Romie's art is a celebration of the human spirit. That is why it moves me.

—Jan Greenberg

School Bell Time, 1978,
Profile/Part I: The Twenties
series, collage on board,
29 1/4 x 41 inches,
private collection

Important Dates

1911 September 2, Romare Howard Bearden was born in Charlotte, North Carolina. His parents were Richard Howard and Bessye Johnson Bearden.

1914–15 Bearden family moves to Harlem in New York City.

1920–21 Lives with his grandmother, Cattie Bearden, in Pittsburgh, Pennsylvania.

1929 Graduates from high school in Pittsburgh.

1935 Graduates from New York University with a B.S. degree in education. Has cartoons published in various magazines.

1936–37 Studies drawing and painting with the artist George Grosz at the Art Students League in New York and joins an association with other African American artists in Harlem.

1938 Begins job as a caseworker for the New York City Welfare Department to serve there off and on for the next thirty years.

1940 Has a studio in Harlem and begins painting scenes mostly based on his childhood memories of the South.

1942 Enlists in the U.S. Army.

1944 First solo exhibit, at G. Place Gallery, Washington, D.C.

1945 Honorably discharged from the army as a sergeant after World War II. Exhibit at Samuel M. Kootz Gallery in New York City. *He is Arisen*, first painting sold to the Museum of Modern Art, New York.

1946–48 Two solo exhibitions in New York City.

1950 Moves to Paris and travels in Europe. He is funded by the G.I. Bill.

1951 Returns to New York, paints a little, and writes and publishes popular songs. Admitted to the hospital with a nervous breakdown. Recovers not long afterward. Meets and marries Nanette Rohan and begins to paint again.

1956 Moves into an apartment/studio on Canal Street in New York City. Painting in an abstract style.

1961 Introduces figures into his painting. Has several solo exhibits in New York City.

1963 Forms Spiral group with other African American artists. Begins making photomontages.

1964 Arne Ekstrom sees his photomontages and mounts an exhibition, including the Projection Series at his gallery, Cordier and Ekstrom, Inc., New York.

1965 Solo exhibition of Projections at Corcoran Gallery, a museum in Washington, D.C.
Receives a grant from the National Institute of Arts and Letters.
Officially retires from New York City welfare department.

1969 Coauthors *The Painter's Mind* with Carl Holty.

1971 "Romare Bearden: The Prevalence of Ritual," retrospective exhibition organized by the Museum of Modern Art, New York.

1972 Elected to the National Institute of Arts and Letters.
Publishes with Harry Henderson, *Six Black Masters of American Art.*

1973 Goes to the island of St. Martin in the Caribbean, where he and Nanette eventually build a house.

1974–78 Has six solo exhibitions of his work (five at Cordier and Ekstrom, Inc., New York).

1980–82 Three solo exhibits at Cordier and Ekstrom, Inc., New York.
"Romare Bearden:1970–1980," a retrospective at the Mint Museum in Charlotte, North Carolina, where Bearden was born.

1983–84 Designs a metro line mural for Baltimore, Maryland.
Designs a mural for the Pittsburgh Independent Train Transit System.
Three solo exhibits at Cordier and Ekstrom, Inc., New York.

1986 "Romare Bearden: Origins and Progressions," a retrospective at the Detroit Institute of Arts, Detroit, Michigan.
Solo exhibit at Cordier and Ekstrom, Inc., New York.

1988 Solo exhibition at the North Carolina Museum of Art, Raleigh, North Carolina.
Bearden dies of bone cancer on March 12.

1989 "Romare Bearden: A Memorial Exhibition" of works from 1941–1988 at ACA Galleries, New York.

1993 Pantheon publishes *A History of African-American Artists: From 1792 to Present,* coauthored with Harry Henderson.

2003–2004 The Art of Romare Bearden, a retrospective exhibition at the National Gallery of Art in Washington, D.C., traveling to the San Francisco Museum of Modern Art; the Dallas Museum of Art; and the Whitney Museum of American Art, New York, New York.

Bibliography

Printed Matter

Romare Bearden. Papers:1933–79. Archives of American Art, Smithsonian Institution, Washington, D.C.

Berman, Avis. "Romare Bearden: 'I Paint out of the Tradition of the Blues'." *Art News:* December 1980.

Brenson, Michael. "Art: Romare Bearden, 'Rituals of the Obeah'." *New York Times*, November 30, 1984.

———. "Romare Bearden: Epic Emotion, Intimate Scale." *New York Times*, March 22, 1988, p. 42.

Brown, Kevin, and Nathan I. Huggins (editor). *Romare Bearden*. New York: Chelsea House, 1994.

Campbell, Mary Schmidt and Sharon F. Patton, *"In Memory and Metaphor: The Art of Romare Bearden, 1940–1987."* Exhibition catalog, The Studio Museum in Harlem. New York: Oxford, 1991.

Gelburd, Gail and Thelma Golden. *"Romare Bearden in Black and White: Photomontage Projections, 1964."* Exhibition catalog, Whitney Museum of American Art. New York: Harry N. Abrams, 1997.

Murray, Albert. "The Visual Equivalent of the Blues." In *"Romare Bearden: 1970–80."* Exhibition catalog. Mint Museum, Charlotte, North Carolina 1980.

Payne, Les. "America's Greatest (Overlooked) Artist." *Newsday*, January, 1988, pp. 6–11 and 18–20.

Schwartzman, Myron. *Romare Bearden: His Life and Art*. New York: Harry N. Abrams, 1990.

———. *Romare Bearden: Celebrating the Victory*. New York: Franklin Watts, 1999.

Sims, Lowery Stokes. *Romare Bearden*. New York: Rizzoli International, 1993.

Tompkins, Calvin. "Putting Something Over Something Else." *The New Yorker*, November 28, 1977: pp. 53–58.

Washington, Bunch M. *The Art of Romare Bearden: The Prevalence of Ritual.* New York: Harry N. Abrams, 1973.

Film

Bearden Plays Bearden, produced by New World Cinema, 1980.

One Night Stand, 1974, Of the Blues series, collage, 44 x 50 inches, private collection

Text Notes

Full bibliographical information may be found on page 50.

MS Myron Schwartzman. *Celebrating the Victory*
P Papers: Archives of American Art
LP Les Payne. "America's Greatest (Overlooked) Artist"
CT Calvin Tompkins. "Putting Something Over Something Else"
AM Albert Murray. "The Visual Equivalent of the Blues"
AB Avis Berman. "I Paint out of the Tradition of the Blues"
KB Kevin Brown and Nathan I. Huggins (ed.). *Romare Bearden*
MM Mary Schmidt Campbell and Sharon F. Patton. *In Memory and Metaphor*
MB Michael Brenson. "Romare Bearden: Epic Emotion, Intimate Scale"

p. 8 Description of Romie's love of trains and "I remember my great-grandfather holding me up to see the railroad
   car with the coffin and the flowers and the soldiers." MS p. 25
p. 11 Romare was the "fair-haired boy" of the family... KB p. 27
p. 12 "It doesn't look anything like her..." LP p. 11
p. 22 Spinky was the nickname for Charles Alston, who also grew up to be an artist.
p. 22 "He got to be our friend." CT p. 53
p. 24 "You had to get with the music..." AM p. 20
p. 26 "Putting the photograph in a different space ...." P
p. 28 "she looked like a locomotive coming around a corner." AB p. 64
p. 29 "Why don't you paint me?" "I know what I look like but when you look and find what's beautiful
   in me . . . "; "It got me started thinking about people I knew . . ." AB p. 64
p. 30 "to paint the life of my people as I know it" KB p. 14
p. 34 "Art celebrates a victory . . . ." AB p. 66
p. 37 "continuous finger-snapping head-shaking enjoyment." MM p. 65
p. 37 "Even though you go through these terrible experiences . . ." AB p. 62
p. 37 "I listened and listened . . ." MB p. 42
p. 39 "I think the artist has to be something like a whale . . ." AB p. 65
p. 46 "People begin to come . . . . You are not working like a photographer." LP p. 8
p. 46 "putting something over something else." CT p. 53
Anecdotes about Bearden's life are repeated in many of the above sources. I am particularly indebted to the work
of Avis Berman, Kevin Brown, Calvin Tompkins, Les Payne, and Myron Schwartzman, and to the artist's own
recounting of events as recorded in his papers.

Glossary

Abstract Expressionism was a development in abstract art (art where there is no recognizable subject)
   explored by American artists in the late 1940s and 1950s.
blues is a bittersweet jazz song or dance form heard since the 1920s and developed by African
   American musicians and composers.
collage is a picture made of bits of paper, fabric or any other material stuck or glued to a surface. It was
   first introduced by the artists Pablo Picasso and Georges Braque in 1912 in Paris.
gouache is a type of watercolor that is opaque, which means it does not allow the whiteness of the paper to
   show through the paint.
hot and **cold colors** refer to the intensity of color achieved by the combination of primary colors (red,
   blue, and yellow) into complementary colors. For example, yellow and blue combine to become green.
   Red-orange is a hot color and green-blue is a cold color. Hot and cold colors placed side by side on
   a picture intensify each other.
jazz is a movement in music from the 1920s often associated with African American musicians and composers.
Masonite is a pressed wood board.
photomontage is a collage made up of cut photographs.
segregation is the separation of groups, obliging them to carry on their activities separately.
shading refers to darkening sections of a drawing or painting to convey the form of an object or figure.

Acknowledgments

Many thanks to the wonderful people at the Romare Bearden Foundation who shared their memories of the artist, their library, and their transparencies of his paintings: Diedra Harris-Kelley, niece of Romare and Nanette Bearden; Sheila Rohan, sister of Nanette Bearden; Evelyn Jackson, sister of Nanette Bearden; and Joan Sandler, Director of the Romare Bearden Foundation. I am grateful for the thoughtful suggestions and expertise of Ruth Fine, Curator of "The Art of Romare Bearden," the exhibition at the National Gallery of Art in Washington, D.C., opening September, 2003, and traveling to the San Francisco Museum of Modern Art; the Dallas Museum of Art; and the Whitney Museum of American Art, New York, New York. Thanks always to my thorough editor Howard Reeves, his assistant Linas Alsenas, and art director Becky Terhune. Thanks also to Ed Miller for his vibrant design. A big thank you to my agent George Nicholson and his assistant Paul Rodeen for their continuing support.

Some Places to View Artwork by Romare Bearden:

Massachusetts
Williams College Museum of Art

Michigan
The Detroit Institute of Arts

Missouri
The Saint Louis Art Museum

New York
Albright-Knox Art Gallery, Buffalo
Brooklyn Museum of Art
Memorial Art Gallery of the University of Rochester
The Metropolitan Museum of Art, NYC
The Museum of Modern Art, NYC
Schomburg Center for Research in Black
    Culture, NYC
Whitney Museum of American Art, NYC

North Carolina
Public Library of Charlotte and
    Mecklenburg County
Mint Museum of Art, Charlotte

Ohio
The Cleveland Museum of Art

Washington, D.C.
National Gallery of Art

Text copyright © 2003 Jan Greenberg

All artwork and photographs copyright © 2003 Romare Bearden Foundation, Inc., Licensed by VAGA, New York.

All works of art by Romare Bearden are © Romare Howard Bearden Foundation, Inc./Licensed by VAGA, New York, NY

Designed by Edward Miller

Library of Congress Cataloging-in-Publication Data

Greenberg, Jan,
Romare Bearden: collage of memories / by Jan Greenberg.
    p. cm.
Summary: Recounts the life of the twentieth-century African-American collage artist who used his southern childhood, New York City, jazz, and Paris to influence his bold and meaningful art.
Includes bibliographical references and index.
  ISBN 0-8109-4589-4
1. Bearden, Romare, 1911-1988—Juvenile literature. 2. African-American artists—United States—Biography—Juvenile literature. [1. Bearden, Romare, 1911-1988. 2. Artists. 3. African Americans–Biography.] I. Bearden, Romare, 1911-1988. II. Title.

N6537.B4 G74 2003
709'.2–dc21

2002153715

Printed in Hong Kong
10 9 8 7 6 5 4 3 2 1

Harry N. Abrams, Inc.
100 Fifth Avenue
New York, N.Y. 10011
www.abramsbooks.com

Abrams is a subsidiary of
LA MARTINIÈRE
GROUPE

front cover: *Three Folk Musicians*, 1967, collage on canvas on board, 50 x 60 inches, J. L. Hudson Gallery, Michigan

back cover: *Eden Noon*, 1988, collage and watercolor, 40 x 30 inches, Estate of Romare Bearden

title page: *Morning*, 1979 lithograph, 21½ x 27 inches, private collection